HARDSHIPS
TO
Blessings

COLTEN J. SKINNER

outskirts
press

Outskirts Press, Inc.
http://www.outskirtspress.com

ISBN: 978-1-9772-3994-5

"Life isn't a destination, it's a journey. We all come upon un-expected curves and turning points. Everything that happens to us shapes who we are becoming. And in the adventure of each day, we discover the important things in life and why they're important."

When I say the word LIFE, what does that mean to you? The word life has different meanings to everyone, but to me the word life means blessings and hardships. I have seen God turn my hardships into amazing blessings, one by one. In this book you will learn how my faith in God, the people He placed in my life along the way, and my outlook on life has changed my hardships into blessings.

TABLE OF CONTENTS

Foreword   i
Chapter 1: Living with A-T   1
Chapter 2: Blessings in Disguise   4
Chapter 3: Obstacles Taken Away   7
Chapter 4: Cancer Sucks   12
Chapter 5: From Strangers to Friends   19
Chapter 6: Dreams Do Come True   23
Chapter 7: Kids Shouldn't Have Cancer   30
Chapter 8: Fun in Chicago   36
Chapter 9: Inspiration   39
Chapter 10: Cancer Never Quits   41
Chapter 11: Friends and Fun   47
Chapter 12: TB12, The G.O.A.T.   53
Chapter 13: American Cancer Society   56
Chapter 14: A Super Experience   62
Chapter 15: Friends and Family Are Everything   68
Chapter 16: Accomplishments   75
Epilogue   78
About the Author   80
Kim Skinner's Tribute   84
Testimonials   86

Foreword

At the age of twenty-eight years, Colten James Skinner understands how precious life is and the importance of living it to the fullest. Born with Ataxia Telangiectasia, a debilitating genetic disorder, Colten values life and celebrates each day as a "gift from God." He is both a blessing and an inspiration to all who know him. His passion and faith are illuminated by personal glimpses of his relationships with family members, friends, his love for sports and his unfailing commitment to his Lord and Savior Jesus Christ.

I have known Colten since birth and watched as his mother Kim faithfully brought both he and his older brother Duey Jordan to church each Sunday. It was heartwarming to see the boys grow in the Lord and to see them grow in their faith under the guiding hand of a loving mother who never tired of devoting time and unconditional love to her sons. His love of the Lord is manifested in his attitude, his ambition and his actions. Colten faithfully attended the Sunday School Class I taught at First Baptist Church and it was with great joy I witnessed his spiritual growth.

In his book, Colten asks his readers to ponder what the word "life" means to them. He candidly shares how hardships in his life evolved into amazing blessings. He shares his most intimate feelings and fears and acknowledges God's amazing blessings which has strengthened and guided him in his life's journey.

Colten has not allowed the infirmities of his body to defeat him, but rather, he has used them to bless and inspire others. He acknowledges God's divine providence and unexpected blessings throughout his life. You will enjoy the quotes and quips that are sprinkled throughout the book and, at the conclusion, you will have a greater appreciation for the "gift of life" and seriously ponder his question "What does the word life mean to you?"

~ Linda J. Crotchett

Chapter 1

LIVING WITH A-T

I WAS BORN in the spring of 1992, in a small town in Illinois. My family consisted of my mom, my brother, and my dad. At birth I was diagnosed with a rare disease called Ataxia Telangiectasia. Doctors previously had diagnosed my brother, Duey Jordan, with the same disease when he was three years old. From this diagnosis on our lives would NEVER be the same!!! Not everyone knows about this disorder, so here are some facts on it: Ataxia Telangiectasia is also called A-T or Louis Barr Syndrome. It is a rare genetic neuro-muscular disorder that destroys part of the motor control area in the brain, leading to a lack of balance and coordination. It also weakens the immune system. A-T gets its name from the combination of two recognizable abnormalities: Ataxia (lack of muscle control) and Telangiectasia (abnormal dilation of capillary vessels that often result in tumors and red skin lesions). A-T also involves extreme sensitivity to radiation and blood cancers such as leukemia and lymphoma.

Researchers named the gene ATM for A-T mutated. Subsequent research revealed that ATM has a significant role in regulating cell division. A-T is very rare, but it occurs worldwide. It is believed that many A-T cases, particularly those who die at a young age are never properly diagnosed. Therefore, this disease may actually be more prevalent. Carriers of one copy of this gene do not develop A-T, but have an increased risk of getting cancer. This puts both of my parents at greater risk. This makes the A-T gene one of the most important cancer-related genes identified to date. The A-T disease occurs only if a defective gene is inherited from both parents.

As infants my brother and I appeared very healthy. At age two, ataxia and nervous system abnormalities began to become apparent. We were very determined, even at a young age, NOT to let this disorder get the best of us. We kept pushing ourselves. When we were infants the doctors had told our parents that they did not expect us to live past the age of 10. Boy did we prove them wrong!

I can do all things through Him who gives me strength.
Philippians 4:13

Today, I am 28. My brother was 29 years old when he passed. When we were young we could both walk, run, write… do what other kids our age could do. That soon changed. Our walk became wobblier and we became more reliant on others and our wheelchairs. We were both eventually confined to wheelchairs for the rest of our lives. My brother got his first wheelchair in 4th grade. I was not far behind that. I got my first wheelchair in the 6th grade. At first it was kind of cool. We were the only kids in our school in wheelchairs. Everyone wanted to push us. Soon we did not like it at all. We felt isolated. We could not do things or go places that our friends went. However, we made the most out of everything we had. It did not take long for us to get accustomed to our new "rolling" way of life. Life is ours for the taking. We can go through life bitter or we can make the most out of what we have. We have to create a life for ourselves that makes us feel good on the inside. Du and I chose to live each day to its fullest. We did not let our wheelchairs keep us from what we wanted to do or go places we wanted to go. We just had to go about things differently.

Colten Skinner and Duey Jordan Skinner

Chapter 2

BLESSINGS IN DISGUISE

If you seek God…Blessings will seek you.
Joel Osteen

BLESSINGS CAN COME in many ways. Some of my blessings began with two people who were, in themselves, blessings in disguise. They did not even know it. There is an Ataxia Telangiectasia Clinic out in Baltimore, Maryland. It is located at Johns Hopkins Hospital. My brother and I began going out there about every five years for appointments. One day at my mom's work, one of her co-workers, Marsha Buis, and herself were talking about and looking over our initial appointment information that we received in the mail. A customer, Carol Yocom, overheard them talking. She came over to my mom and said her niece, Tammi Miller, worked at Johns Hopkins Hospital. Carol said Tammi was coming for a visit the following week. Our appointments were scheduled over our school's Thanksgiving break. When Tammi was in Jerseyville, she helped us arrange our trip. This took a lot of stress off of my mom. My aunt Dawn went with us to help my mom push my brother and me in our wheelchairs. She goes most places with us. We kept in touch on our drive out there. Tammi said, she, her husband Mike, and their two daughters, Katie and Lindsay, would meet us for dinner at ESPN ZONE - a sports bar and grill. A few minutes after we got to the hotel room, Tammi called and told us that there were some football players hanging out in the restaurant. We tried to get there before they left, but my mom took a wrong turn. We soon found out you do not want to make a wrong turn in Baltimore. There are lots of one-way streets. If we could have walked there we would have probably gotten there quicker! Soon enough though we would make it to "ESPN ZONE" for dinner. When we finally got there Mike said that we had just missed the football players. I would have liked to see them, but it did not matter, we had a great time. The Millers were really nice. It felt like we had been friends forever even though we just had met. I believe that people are put in one's life for a reason. This family still remains a blessing to me over the years.

The next day our appointments at Johns Hopkins Hospital began. The doctors and staff were wonderful. We had a few days of appointments being seen by an immunologist, a neurologist, a pulmonologist, and a nutritionist/dietician. They were impressed how well we were doing. Because of their encouraging words, Du and I were now more determined than ever to keep plugging along. I understand that words are strong. I want to be sure to speak kind words, words of praise, or words of encouragement today and every day to someone else. I never know: I might just change someone's life. Mom and dad taking really good care of us changed our life; in addition, I think our determination fueled by others, our faith, and trust in God has brought us this far.

Chapter 3

OBSTACLES TAKEN AWAY

As my brother and I grew older, we became more and more dependent on our wheelchairs. With this dependency, obstacles were arising. We had a minivan, but it was not equipped for our power wheelchairs. Due to this we could only take our manual wheelchairs when we went anywhere. With this being said, we were reliant on others to push us most of the time. Our church family at First Baptist Church in Jerseyville, Illinois, decided that they were not going to allow that my brother and I had to be so dependent on others. They decided to have a chili supper with all proceeds going towards a wheelchair accessible van. A church member and good family friend, Kim Marshall, spear headed everything. At a later date, Kim and other friends and church members, Tim and Kaye Buis, organized an auction that was held at the American Legion Fairgrounds in Jerseyville. This was a community wide event. We had thousands of items donated. Quite a few church members were involved in carrying out this event. Collecting and organizing it all took days. The actual auction took us all day and late into the evening to finally finish. In addition to these money making endeavors, our school, Jersey Community High School, had "donate for doughnut days" fundraisers. These fundraising events were so much fun! Don't get me wrong, these events were not all fun and games all the time. They took a lot of time and hard work. Kim Marshall is the owner of Marshall Chevy Buick GMC in Jerseyville, Illinois. She contacted and made arrangements with the GMC plant in Wentzville, Missouri for us to have a full-size wheelchair accessible van made. We got to go tour the plant and actually follow our van down the assembly line. At the end of the day, the GMC plant gave my brother and I a miniature version of our van. When our van was finished, United Access in St. Louis, Missouri added the wheelchair lift and mobility tie-downs for us. They helped us apply for a mobility grant, which we were granted! Between selling our previous minivan, the fundraisers, and the grant, our new ride was completely paid for. We were now on our way to a new life with less limitations. Such a blessing!

> *"At the end of the day, I am thankful that*
> *my blessings are bigger than my problems."*
> Henri Fredric Amiel

Another hardship we were living with was actually one we were living *in*. Our home! It was old and definitely not wheelchair accessible, which made it extremely difficult to get around.

This was a huge obstacle as we could not use our wheelchairs. We were either helped with our walking, carried, given piggy back rides, or we crawled when we needed to get somewhere. Depending upon how tired our legs and arms were determined our mode of transportation. One day, Duey Jordan's aide from school, Patty Saettele, decided to contact a home makeover television show. She sent them everything they needed. In the end we were not chosen. This was a huge disappointment not only for us, but for Patty, our friends, and family, as well. Our community, family, friends, and church members were determined by now to get us into a wheelchair accessible home. They would unite as one and build us a beautiful wheelchair accessible home. Since we were not chosen for the home makeover show, they decided we would have our own version of the television show. No camera crew or television personalities would be there. Our version was so much better! Our local newspaper, Jersey County Journal, covered the project. We had our own personal reporter, Jill Thurston. She interviewed us and it seemed like she wrote a story just about every week focusing on my brother Du and me. My brother and I loved this. We felt like we were celebrities. Everyone knew who we were. We thought we knew a lot of people, but we were about to meet a lot more. Total strangers to our family volunteered to help in any way they could. Businesses and organizations also helped. When I say it was a community endeavor, I mean it! Hundreds played an important role by- donating money, donating supplies, physical labor, cooking for the workers, running errands, taking pictures, and clean up.

The fundraising began again. A lot of time and energy was spent making each fundraiser a success. Kim Marshall organized a "Deal or No Deal" evening. The employees at her dealership worked this event. Bill Erwin was the "Host" and Craig Billings was the "Banker." Others took care of tables as a dinner was prepared and served by the Hayes family. The Jersey Community High School cheerleaders were the 26 case holders. That evening was a blast!! We had so much fun, everyone made us feel so special! We had 250 people in attendance. They were not there for all the delicious food and a good time, but for **us**. This is what life is all about…helping and caring for others. I learned at an early age, the Golden Rule: "Do unto others as you would have others do unto you." I can honestly say my hometown lives by this rule.

Another act of kindness was the "Duck Race" hosted by Joe and Jan DeSherlia at their Marina on the Mississippi River in Grafton, Illinois. There were hundreds of rubber ducks in a roped off area. People would buy a duck hoping theirs would be the first to cross the finish line. This was a crazy fun time. Some of our friends whom we hadn't seen for a while showed up at the event. Fundraising events seem to bring out the best in everyone, from the attendees that come to the events, organizations that sponsor your events, and the donations from individuals and businesses.

As the recipients of these fundraising events, we were humbled and blessed! When our house was done, my brother and I felt like our lives had changed. We finally did not have to wait to get help to go from room to room anymore. We were now independent instead of being so dependent on others. When people come together…great things happen.

Alone we can do so little, together we can do so much.
Helen Keller

Susan Allen, Patty Saettele. Duey and Colten Skinner
with their new wheelchair accessible van.

Turn your worries into praise and watch
God turn them into blessings.
Unknown

Chapter 4

CANCER SUCKS

*Be strong and courageous. Do not be afraid or terrified
because of them, for the Lord your God goes with
you; He will never leave you nor forsake you.*
Deuteronomy 31:6

*He has promised, no matter the situation, He will
never leave us. No matter our fear, He is with us.*
Unknown

I WAS SO excited to move into our new wheelchair accessible
home. I had a lot of unpacking to do before getting settled in
my new room. I was going through life like any other teenager
should when cancer struck. But let me start from the beginning.
It was a Saturday afternoon in May of 2009. I was attending

my friend's, Jordan Buis, graduation party. My right side began hurting me while I was there. I did not get to stay but about an hour. We went to the doctor the next week thinking I was just experiencing a sore muscle from transferring in and out of my wheelchair. My pediatrician checked me for a bladder infection/UTI. The results came back negative. He too came to the same conclusion that I probably had bumped my side or pulled a muscle transferring in and out of my wheelchair. During the following week the pain in my side traveled up into my chest. My doctor had always been hesitant about X-rays with my Ataxia Telangiectasia. He felt it was necessary to order a chest X-ray to check for possible pneumonia. The X-ray showed no signs of pneumonia, for which we were thankful. However, the X-ray did reveal a mass in my chest. What? Could it be Cancer? This possible diagnosis of cancer was the furthest thing imaginable. My doctor sent me directly to the Emergency Room at Children's Hospital in St. Louis, Missouri. This is where they gave us the horrible, but true news that I did in fact have cancer. Non-Hodgkin's Lymphoma was the diagnosis. A cancer diagnosis is very scary and overwhelming. I remember my cancer diagnosis vividly. I remember being told "YOU HAVE CANCER." It was terrible, I thought it was the end for me. I was only 16 years old and my life was ending. How could this happen? Then in that same instant when my world came to a sudden halt, a sense of peace came over me as if someone was telling me, "You can do this, I will help you." At that point I knew my cancer was in God's hands and He was in control. Even though I did not know just how He would, I had relief knowing that He could! I did not know what to expect. Was I going to die or were the doctors and nurses going to be able to help me? They sent me immediately to the Intensive Care Unit (ICU). I was there for what seemed like forever. Just lying there hooked up to all kinds of machines and tubes. It was scary. Not a roller-coaster or a horror movie scary, but scary knowing that I was helpless and I could do nothing about it.

> *Tough times don't last, tough people do.*
> Robert Schuller

My friend, Jordan, and my brother, Duey Jordan, went down to the hospital cafeteria to get something to eat while they were visiting me in the ICU one evening. Everyone says my brother and I look alike. I don't see it. One of my nurses saw them and thought it was me trying to escape. Remember my brother uses a wheelchair, as well. Everyone thought this was funny. Something else that was funny was when I was having lots of pain, I was given morphine. So everything was hilarious to me. I mean everything! My doctor's name was Dr. Doctor. The pastor of my church at the time was Pastor Church. Pastor came over to the hospital to see me. My mom introduced them. We all immediately started laughing. Pastor Church, Dr. Doctor and myself would talk about funny names like that for what seemed like hours. I don't remember who said it, but one of them said they knew a dentist, Dr. Yankum. It was stuff like that that would get me to laugh and take my mind off of cancer.

I liked my nurse in ICU. She was very nice, fun to talk with, and very pretty. I had a bunch of monitors on me telling the nurse how fast my heart was beating, what my oxygen level was and some took pictures of parts of my body. If you know me, you know that I'm really ornery I would take the stickers off my body so she would have to come in and stick them back on. This would happen "on accident," I would tell her. The truth is, it was on purpose. When I was stable enough I was sent to the 9th floor with all the other cancer patients. Even though I was in a children's hospital I was really nervous. The first nurse that came in my room on the in-patient side of the 9th floor was Amanda. She told me she lived near me in Jerseyville. I immediately felt at ease. This was a blessing. I did not know her. I think out of all of the nurses that could have been assigned to me, it was God's plan for us to meet. I was not worried anymore. I knew I could trust her to take excellent care of me, which she did. We are now friends. This is where I spent most of the next two years of my life, in and out of Children's Hospital. Twice a week, sometimes even three times a week, I would have to go to the clinic side of the 9th floor to get my chemo treatments. Those usually took all day. I had a wonderful nurse, Leslie, in clinic for most of my visits. She is very pretty and nice to talk to. We have also become friends. Having two years of chemotherapy she had gotten to know me really well. The rest of the time was spent in-patient.

Life happens. Adapt. Embrace change, and make
the most of everything that comes your way.
Nick Jonas

I missed my new home that we had recently moved into. I missed my bed, my dogs, and most of all I missed seeing all my friends and family. I made some new friends in the hospital though. Most of them I still talk with. They were like my second family: the doctors, nurses, housekeepers, and fellow patients. I could have visitors, but it just didn't feel like home. One day I was getting really tired of being there in the hospital, I had had enough! I was grouchy and annoying to my nurse. She came in when I wasn't expecting it and squirted me with water out of her syringe and said, "Take that." We both started laughing. That was the most excitement I had in a while. I realized then that the doctors and nurses weren't there to make my life miserable or to hurt me, they were there to help cure me and to have some fun along the way.

Quite often my blood counts would go down and I would develop a fever. Sadly, this kept occurring and I would have to be admitted into the hospital. This was my new way of life, my new reality, my new home away from home. I had to accept it. Some stays were longer than others. For me being at a hospital was very scary, even though my mom was with me most of the time. When she couldn't be with me, my dad, grandmas, my aunt Dawn, or my aunt Kim would be. Being at a Children's Hospital had its benefits. They have movies to watch, they play games with you, they played music and sang songs, just to mention a few things. Since I was a teenager at the time, most of the nurses were just a few years older than me, so I liked talking with them. I played a lot of video games and watched movies in my spare time. I went through two years of chemotherapy, port accesses, CT Scans, MRI's, spinal taps, blood draws, fluid bags, blood transfusions, and a whole bunch of overnight hospital stays. These were all hardships that I encountered along my life's journey.

> *I am never in control of what happens around me, but*
> *I am always in control of what happens within me.*
> Unknown

When I received the great news after two long, harsh, awful years that my cancer was in remission, I was so happy and proud of myself. Praise God!!

> *Let your faith be bigger than your fears.*
> Tom Trenney

God never puts you through anything He doesn't think you can't handle. He was always alongside me. He will always bring you out stronger and that He did! The nurses in the cancer clinic had a little party for me and I got to ring the bell. It was an awesome feeling that I had beat cancer. Today, I am very proud to say I am a cancer survivor! It was because I wasn't a whiner, I was a warrior. The biggest reason is my never ending faith in God.

> *"Many will start fast; few will finish strong."*
> Gary Ryan Blair

If you believe you can do something you can. God will never give up on you. All you have to do is put your faith in God and trust Him. He will turn your hardships into many blessings.

Colten Skinner offering some inspiration
during the Hope Bowl in Boston.

Chapter 5

FROM STRANGERS TO FRIENDS

OUR FRIENDS, THE Millers, from Baltimore, Maryland had two tickets to game three of the 2013 World Series in St. Louis, Missouri at Busch Stadium. The St. Louis Cardinals vs. the Boston Red Sox! They could not go due to an illness of a friend/ neighbor. They called us to see if we would want the tickets. Mike and Tammi wanted my mom to take my brother (he is a huge St. Louis Cardinals fan), but it was a night game and he did not like night games. My mom and I would go to the game. I am a huge Boston Red Sox fan. Our tickets were supposed to be just up from the field. The stadium crew said there was no way they could get me down there, so they sat mom and I on the main level with the camera man behind home plate. What happens next was another blessing in disguise. Before the game started this woman dressed up from head to toe in Red Sox gear wearing a replica of Fenway Park on her head walked up our way. Me being the outgoing person that I am yelled out to her, "Hey Fenway Park Hat Lady." She and her husband came right over to us. I just wanted a picture with her. I did not know it yet, but she would give a lot more. They introduced themselves as Lynne and Gary Smith. My mom would introduce herself and then me as the "Red Sox number one fan." The lady quickly corrected my mom and said *she* was the "Red Sox number one fan." That she was we soon found out. We talked for a while and she wrote down my email address. Before she went to her seat she said she would be in touch. The game soon started. A once in a lifetime opportunity to be attending a World Series Game. Such a blessing! It was a fun night and a good game. When my mom and I left, neither one of us thought we would be contacted by this woman I called the "Fenway Park Hat Lady." We were wrong! We were contacted by her a couple months later. First, I got an email from her asking if I would like to come out to Boston, Massachusetts. All we would have to do is pay for our airfare. She would take care of the rest, food, hotel, rides to and from places, etc. She said I could pick out a three game series at Fenway Park. I was getting excited, so I called my mom and told her all about it. She said not to get your hopes up, that it was too good to be true. Boy were we wrong!

The next day, we received a call from a woman. The woman was Lynne. She left us a lengthy message saying that her and her husband, Gary, would talk with people and arrange everything if we would like to come out to Boston. Total strangers were asking us to fly out to the East coast and trust everything to them.

There are no strangers, only friends you haven't met yet.
William Butler Yeats

Well, we did! They arranged everything from hotel stays, limo service, dining, baseball game tickets, and lots of surprises along the way. It's nice to know there are good people in the world. We all need to be nice to each other.

Life is 10 percent what happens to you
and 90 percent how you react to it.
Charles Swindoll

I was so excited I called my best friend, Brayden Morris, to come along with my mom and me. We waited for months for the day to come that we were on our way to Boston. We spoke with Lynne often leading up to our trip. She would tell my mom and I some information, however, she kept lots of secrets. My friend, Brayden, and I would call/text each other about weekly and talk about our upcoming trip. Neither one of us could wait, especially me!

It's hard to wait around for something you
know may never happen, but it's harder when
you know it's everything you want.
Unknown

This trip to Fenway Park in Boston is something I had dreamed of and wished for since I was in grade school. It was soon to become a reality. Whoever says dreams do not come true is wrong. I am so glad that I got to experience this dream with my childhood best friend, Brayden Morris. Such a blessing! When we arrived in Boston, there was a man by a really nice black Yukon holding a sign that read, "Welcome to Boston, Colten Skinner." Many emotions came to me at this moment, joy, happiness, and excitement rushed through me all at once. Our drive to the hotel only took about 25 minutes, but it felt like an hour for me. I wanted to get there so bad. Our driver was awesome. He showed us interesting places and historic buildings along the way to our hotel. When we got to our room, much to my surprise, there was a bag of goodies from the hotel and a card that had my name on it. We put our bags down and I began looking in my goodie bag. Not two minutes later there was a knock on the door. Guess who it was? Yes, it was Lynne and Gary who had a couple of bags jam packed full of Red Sox stuff. All that was for me! We did not have much time to relax in the hotel room before we were on to the next fun and exciting part of our four-day trip. The fun had just begun! Lynne and Gary are awesome! They provided me with an *unforgettable* Boston experience.

Gary and Lynne Smith

Chapter 6

~

DREAMS DO COME TRUE

No dream is too big, when you understand
ABUNDANCE is your birthright.
Unknown

I HAD NEVER been to historic Fenway Park before but had always dreamed of going there one day. That day had come! In the summer of 2014, it was everything that I had ever dreamed and thought it would be and then more. The first day spent at Fenway Park was busier than the other two days, but of course all three were really fun. Lynne took us in the stadium before it opened to the public for a tour. We went places that only a select few have ever gone. I felt like a very important person! Blessed! After our private tour I received a big surprise. Someone from the Boston Red Sox locker room came out with a baseball glove. It was Jon Lester's glove. He is my favorite pitcher! It was autographed and had a personal inscription which read, "Never Give Up." Never Give Up is his Charitable Foundation. This meant so much to me. Not only is he my favorite pitcher, but he also had the same cancer as me: Non-Hodgkin's Lymphoma. The person who came out of the Red Sox locker room said that Jon Lester could not bring out the glove to me himself because he was getting ready for the game that night. Then we were taken to the EMC club for dinner. This is behind home plate and high enough up to have a great view of the entire field. It was an elegant, but yet comfortable setting. After we had dinner, I got to try on the World Series rings and get pictures with the World Series Trophies. Awesome! Soon, it was game time. Our seats were fantastic! We were in between home plate and first base. I loved being at Fenway Park for the game. It is so much better than watching the game on television. In the bottom of the 7th inning, the fans have a tradition that they sing along to the song "Sweet Caroline" by Neil Diamond. In the 8th inning we were getting hot so we decided to go to the EMC club to cool off. I'm glad we did! What happened next was unexpected, I had no idea, but I enjoyed every second of it. One of the players' wife's, Lindsay Buchholz, took me by the hand and led us to the player's garage. This is where I finally got to meet Jon Lester and his wife Farrah along with other players, their wives and kids. Jon was the first player to walk in. It was like he knew me. As soon as he walked in the garage he looked right at me and said, "Hello Colten." We would talk for a bit, and I told him that he had the same cancer as I did. He would sign my jersey right where I told him I had my cancer. He told me, "we are connected now." Our paths would cross again later, in Chicago. Then the other players started coming in. I got all the players to sign my jersey and I had my picture taken with each one of them. It's a good thing I wore my white jersey. I was going to wear my navy jersey. Signatures wouldn't have shown up on that jersey. When we got back to our hotel room I could not stop talking about the day/night I just had. It did not matter to me that my team lost. It was just day one of my four-day trip to the Boston/Foxboro area. I did not know how it could get any better than this. But IT DID!

Games two and three were not as busy as Friday. Saturday was an evening game and Sunday was an afternoon game. Sunday was Father's day. On the way to Fenway Park, we ran into these big, green, friendly, monsters, the Red Sox mascots: "Wally"; his sister, "Tessie"; their mother, "Wanda"; and father, "Walter." Then, we went and met former player and World Series pitcher, Tim Wakefield. We talked until it was time for him to start the pregame broadcast. I then was on my way to have brunch with a player. I had no clue who the player was. All I knew was what Gary told me, his name started with the letter "J". When he came into the room I was super excited. It was Jonny Gomes! My mom was even excited she thought he was "hot". We had a Q&A session followed up by an autograph session and pictures. I also got to meet the Red Sox Poet Laureate and organist at Fenway Park, Dick Flavin. He let me put on his World Series rings, he was a very nice man. Before he had to go get ready for the game, he read some poem's out of his book, "Red Sox Rhymes, Verses, and Curses." There was one that stuck out to me. It was to the tune of "Take Me Out to The Ballgame." His version had a different spin to it. It went like this:

"Take me out to the ballgame
First, let's stop at the bank
I'll need a mortgage so I can pay
Parking the car is another outlay
And you pay big bucks for a hotdog
The cost of beer is insane
For it's Oh My! Prices are high
At the old ballgame."

Brayden Morris, Kim Skinner, Colten, Lynne
and Gary Smith at Fenway Park

For a baseball fan like myself, I really enjoyed my private
reading. Next, we were taken on another tour of Fenway. Tours
of Fenway Park never get old. You always see something new

and learn something you didn't know before. This tour led us outside. We got to go inside the Green Monster (a 37-foot-tall wall) for a picture and we got to watch batting practice. Then, it was game time. During the game I got two final surprises from the Red Sox. The first was our names displayed on the big screen, it read: Welcome to Fenway Park Colten, Brayden, and Kim. The next surprise was an autographed baseball bat from my favorite slugger, David Ortiz (Big Papi). We even took a selfie! The next day we had to get up early to go to the airport, or so I thought.

I did not know where we were going. We had been driving for a while. We drove past the entrance to Gillette Stadium. This is where my favorite football team, the New England Patriots, play. I did not realize I was in the parking lot. It was huge. Roadways and parking everywhere. I made the comment, "I really want to come here." My mom just said, "maybe someday." All of a sudden, we came to a stop in front of Gillette Stadium. I realized then I was really there! There is an area at the stadium called "Patriot Place." Patriot Place is like a little town. It has a bunch of stores, numerous restaurants, a movie theater, a bowling alley, and a couple of hotels. Great place! Lynne, Gary, and their son met us there. This is where we all met another soon to be good friend, Donna Spigarolo. Donna is the Director of Community Relations at New England Patriots. She and the Smith's had never met before, only talked on the phone about me. It is amazing how people's lives become intertwined. We all ate lunch together at a restaurant, Davio's. Really good food by the way! We were treated like royalty. We had our own private dining room and waiter. This is where another dream of mine came true: I got to put an *official* Super Bowl ring on my finger! Yes! My finger! Can you believe it? My finger has had World Series and Super Bowl rings on it! Awesome!

After lunch was over, Donna took all of us to The Hall at Patriot Place. This is a big building celebrating Patriots Hall of Famers with old pictures, memorabilia, interactive activities, and movies to watch. After we spent some time in "The Hall," Donna took us all onto the field. We stopped at the 50-yard line. All I could think about was this is where Tom Brady stands. Then I was presented with a football jersey, not any jersey, my favorite player, Tom Brady's jersey. Autographed! I was like a little kid. I flipped out of my wheelchair and did snow angels or grass angels because there was no snow on the field where my favorite team plays. When we were finished taking pictures on the field it was time to head to our limo. When I looked back on the field I could see *my tracks* from *my wheelchair*. How blessed I am! The Patriots' rookies came walking out of the tunnel as we passed. They were tall and looked very strong. We had to stop of course. I got to shake all of their hands and they introduced themselves. Very nice and polite guys! We even got to take a few group pictures. I guess you could say I just happened to be in the right place at the right time, or was it another case of fate? Remember, after all, this book is about my life being filled with blessings!

Hardships often prepare ordinary people
for extraordinary destiny's
CS Lewis

Colten with Brett Sawin and Donna Spigarolo
at Gillette Stadium in Foxboro, Massachusetts

Chapter 7

KIDS SHOULDN'T
HAVE CANCER

Colten with Jonny Wade at Relay for Life
in Jerseyville, Illinois

MAY 2015, I participated in a cancer walk that was being held at Jersey Community Hospital Wellness Center. I was a cancer survivor so I felt driven to walk in it (or in my case roll). For those of you who have not participated in a cancer walk, I encourage you to check into it. It is a fun day-long event and at the same time you are helping fund a cure for cancer. So someday no one will have to go through the harsh cancer treatments like my dear brother Duey Jordan, myself, and my little friend, Jonny Wade have done. I went to church with Jon, Kimberly, Jacky, and Jonny Wade. I did not know them very well before, but we got to know each other better beginning that night. They were there because Jon was the CEO of the hospital and one of the twins, Jonny, had cancer. Jonny had a rare brain tumor. He went to be with the Lord on Christmas Eve, 2015. He was only 8 years old and he passed away in his mother's arms. It was just a year after being diagnosed. Jonny was a sweet boy. When he was in the hospital he would tell his mother, "I don't want any other kid to have cancer." Can we just think about this for a minute! For an 8-year-old to say something like that is just selfless. His mother, Kimberly, started a foundation after Jonny's death in memory of him. This foundation is called, Kids Shouldn't Have Cancer Foundation. I have been active in helping raise money to honor his selfless wish that no other kid should have cancer. This was his wish so it is the foundations mission.

The Kids Shouldn't Have Cancer Foundation (501c3) was founded in memory of Jonny Wade, shortly after brain cancer took his life at the age of 8. Despite the circumstances, Jonny believed he could – and should – make a difference for other children affected by cancer. This is Jonny's foundation. We honor his faith and strength by carrying forward his wish as our mission, that no other kid should have cancer. Our mission statement is: "To conquer pediatric cancer through research and political action with emphasis on responsible spending." By the way, did you know cancer is the leading cause of disease-related death for kids younger than 15 in the United States? Pediatric cancer research is vastly underfunded by the federal government and mostly ignored in pharmaceutical research. We need to do more for kids like Jonny! The National Cancer Institute allots only a small percent of its budget for childhood cancers. Funding for other pediatric diseases is also scarce. This cannot stand!

Here is a little of Jonny's story. In December of 2014, Jonny was looking forward to Christmas with the anticipation and excitement you would expect from a 7-year-old. He lived in Jerseyville, Illinois, with his parents, twin brother Jacky, and the family dog, Lucy. He loved first grade, spending time with his many friends and playing video games with Jacky. A week before Christmas, Jonny got a headache at school. It went away, but it was bad enough that he mentioned it at home. His headache came back and continued. Then it got worse. In the span of just eight days, he was diagnosed with a malignant brain tumor. Just days after Christmas, Jonny underwent a five-hour brain surgery to remove as much of the tumor as possible. Over the next year, Jonny endured four more brain surgeries, as well as eye surgeries, surgical port accesses, feeding tube insertions, radiation therapy, and more scans and needle sticks than the family could count. He constantly had tubes in his nose, chest and, later, in his belly. For more information, I invite you to go to our website www.kidsshouldnthavecancer.org. I volunteered my time as a member of this group shortly after Jonny's passing. It made me very sad when he passed. When I met him I felt a connection. I love helping people and I had pediatric cancer, so I knew how harsh these drugs can be on one's body. I am on the foundation's sales and marketing committee. We have several fundraising events and foundation merchandise for purchase. Our main fundraising events are annual: A Gala, which takes place in St. Louis, Missouri; Gold Party in Frisco, Texas; and a Fun Run. I have been the recipient of an award at the Gala event that I am very proud of. This award is the Jack Wade Courage Award. This award is for the courage and strength, Jack had for his twin brother Jonny. I got this award for my strength and courage shown for my brother during his cancer treatments. We may not have been twins or even seen eye to eye most of the time, but we loved each other the same way as Jacky and Jonny did. These events are so much fun, even though they break your heart hearing a child's cancer story. If you are interested in attending any of our events, you can go to our website for more information. We also have Kids Shouldn't Have Cancer Foundation merchandise for purchase. There are t-shirts, sweatshirts, can cozies, and more. If you feel inclined to, you could simply just make a monetary donation. From these fundraising events and merchandise sales we have raised over two million dollars for funding, and given five separate significant grants for pediatric cancer research to help save children's lives. We have also spearheaded and passed three separate bills in Congress related

Colten, Mike and Tammi Miller enjoying the Gala

Colten Skinner with foundation members at the Gala

to pediatric cancer research. In January, 2020, we were able to fulfill a critical piece of legislation that Congress allocated $50 million to pediatric cancer research. We introduced into Congress the "Jonny Wade Pediatric Cancer Research Act" for $372 million towards pediatric cancer research. We are focused on our mission of saving all children who suffer from this ever-growing horrible disease. We will not stop until there is a cure, because "Kids Deserve a Cure."

Tough times prove ourselves to God and they build our relationship with Him. It might seem hard, but remember God is on your side.
Fritz Chery, from biblereasons.com

Chapter 8

FUN IN CHICAGO

I HAD ALWAYS wanted to go to a baseball game at historic Wrigley Field in Chicago, Illinois. Another dream of mine was about to happen when my favorite pitcher from the Boston Red Sox, Jon Lester, became a Chicago Cub. My good friends from Boston, Lynne and Gary, knew someone that worked in the Cubs organization. Of course they did, they know everyone! She would organize a meet-and-greet with Jon Lester. I had met him in Boston, but I was so nervous and excited, I did not talk as much as I wished I had. This time would be different! One of Kim Marshall's daughters, Erica, made me a "#1 Jon Lester Fan" Cubs shirt for me to wear to the game. Before long it was my mom, Kim, Stan Hudson (another friend of ours), Brayden, and myself heading to Chicago. None of us had ever ridden on a train before. It was a fun experience for us all. When we arrived we took a cab to our hotel on Michigan Avenue. We had some lunch at Dick's Last Resort, good food and a fun environment. We walked to the Navy Pier. It had a lot of fun things to do including a giant Ferris Wheel. It does not stop for you to get in. You have to get in on the move. However, it was slow enough the workers could help me into it. It was pretty awesome at the top! You could see for miles. The second day was game day. It was a busy one. The first thing we did when we arrived at Wrigley Field is take the tour of the stadium. Our tour guide showed us all around. She took us outside to tell us some history about the stadium and its surroundings. We were even allowed to touch the ivy in center field. For a baseball fan like me this is pretty incredible! Wow! Then, we were taken to a big room with three televisions, a comfy couch and several chairs. We were to wait here to be taken on the field for a special visit with Jon Lester. I was brought a goodie bag while we were waiting. I got to meet several Cubs players and coaches. I even got a few autographs and baseballs from batting practice. Stan and I watched Jon Lester throw for a while before he came over. When he came over he said, "How you doing Colten?" He remembered me from Boston! I was excited, but this time I was not so nervous. I actually talked with him. We talked for about 30 minutes about baseball stuff. I thanked him for the glove he had previously given me in Boston. He asked me if I threw away all my Boston Red Sox gear. I said, "No," of course! The Cubs were playing the Atlanta Braves that weekend. On the way off the field I saw another player that used to play for the Red Sox, A.J. Pierzynski. He was now on the Atlanta Braves. I yelled, A.J., he turned around, came over and talked with me for a while. Then we headed to our awesome seats behind home plate to watch some baseball. Game two was just for us guys. Mom and Kim spent the day shopping on Michigan Avenue. Even though I was not a Cubs or a Braves fan, these games and experiences at Wrigley Field were everything I thought they would be. After the game we all met at the Navy Pier for dinner and an Architectural Boat Tour. I had a great weekend in Chicago!

Colten and Kim Skinner, Kim Marshall,
Stan Hudson, and Brayden Morris

Chapter 9

INSPIRATION

Life is not about finding yourself.
Life is about creating yourself.
George Bernard Shaw

INSPIRATION CAN COME to one in different ways. The baseball player who inspired me with hope and strength while I was going through my cancer treatments and ultimately beating cancer is my favorite pitcher, Jon Lester. For those of you who do not know who Jon Lester is, here is a little background on him. Jonathan Tyler Lester was born January 7, 1984. He is a professional baseball pitcher in the National League with the Chicago Cubs in Major League Baseball (MLB). He previously played for the Boston Red Sox from 2006 to 2014 and the Oakland

Athletics in 2014. Jon Lester was diagnosed at age 22, with Non-Hodgkin's Lymphoma. Jon Lester's bout with cancer had a profound impact on the Boston Red Sox pitcher's life. Lester's whole world changed in 2006 when the left-hander was diagnosed with cancer. Lester returned to the diamond following his successful battle with cancer in July 2007. He earned the victory in the Red Sox's World Series-clinching game later that year, and then tossed a no-hitter in 2008. Lester has enjoyed plenty of success since his cancer diagnosis. Off the field, Jon Lester started the NVRQT or "Never Quit" fundraising campaign to support pediatric cancer research. Because during his cancer he had never quit fighting. My favorite quote from Jon Lester is: "As difficult as cancer was; it was good for me in some ways." Just like Jon, my cancer diagnosis was good for me too, in some ways. Having been diagnosed with cancer has made me look at my life and live my life differently. I now cherish every moment. This is why during my cancer treatments Jon Lester was, and still is, an inspiration for me.

Learn to appreciate the things you have before time makes you appreciate the things you had.
Unknown

Chapter 10

CANCER NEVER QUITS

I would rather walk with God in the
dark, than go alone in the light!
Mary Gardiner Brainard

MY BROTHER HAD always dreamed of going to Washington, D.C. In September of 2017, his dream came true. My mom took him for a week-long trip over his birthday. Little did we know this would be the last trip he would take. He was so excited to finally be in D.C. with all the history and beauty. He and my mom went everywhere and saw what D.C had to offer. They must have put hundreds of miles on Du's wheelchair, as well as, my mom's legs and feet. In college he got his Bachelor's degree in Criminal Justice. He wanted to be employed by the White House or the Pentagon one day. His birthday is September 19th, and he always wanted to go to

Duey Jordan Skinner in Washington, D.C.

the White House. He thought it would be awesome to spend his birthday pretending to be the President in the White House. September 19, 2017, this would become a reality. Du and mom spent the afternoon in the White House. He really liked this! He said he felt like the President because he got all kinds of special treatment. He said it was because he was in a wheelchair. The tour they were on took them up and down stairs. He and our mom got to take the elevator with their own personal tour guide. They got to go places the others didn't. Being in a wheelchair isn't all bad: there are some advantages. When they returned from this trip, in his own words, he described it as the "Best trip ever!" He was still on cloud nine from seeing all the history and everything in Washington D.C. That was soon overshadowed by his diagnosis of Type 1 Diabetes. Not long after that, a devastating diagnosis of pancreatic cancer. Cancer returns to our family.

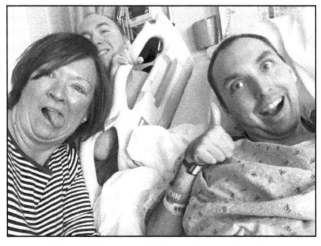

Kim, Colten, and Duey Jordan having
a little bit of fun at the hospital.

Cancer never stops! At first, the doctors just diagnosed him with the Type 1 Diabetes. This was bad enough. He had to get insulin injections, which he hated. My mom hated them, too. She had to give him his injections. He kept getting sick. When he went back to his doctor and they did more tests on him, they found the pancreatic cancer. Devastating news again!

He was put on hospice care 5 months later. I did not get to spend my birthday with him. He was in the hospital. A couple days later my mom had my dad bring me over to stay with her and Du. My brother and best friend, Duey Jordan, passed away on March 26, 2018 just 14 days after my birthday. I was sitting right beside his bed when he took his last breath.

> *You never know how strong you are until*
> *being strong is the only choice you have.*
> Bob Marley

We had always been together. We spent our entire lives side-by-side. This was hard for me because now we were side by side at his death. I do know though, one day Du and I will be together, side by side again in Heaven for eternity. This is God's promise!

> *Grief never ends…but it changes. It is a passage,*
> *not a place to stay. Grief is not a sign of weakness,*
> *nor a lack of faith… it is the price of love.*
> Unknown

My mom, Du, and I should have still been celebrating my birthday month. Instead we were grieving over my brother's death and planning a funeral. Later that night I had a dream that I went to Heaven. I saw God, Jesus, and my brother standing together. God handed me a box. A rectangular shaped, white, box with a glowing around it. As God handed me the box, Du said to me, "Finish It." I have never figured out what was in that shiny, white box, nor have I figured out what my brother wanted me to finish. I woke up when I opened the box. I guess what was in the box was the gift of life and the words "Finish It" meant to go and finish my life - to keep on living. I did not have another dream like this for quite a while. Not for a year to be exact.

The next dream was different. It still took me to Heaven, but this time I was walking with a bearded man in a white robe. It was so beautiful up there, like paradise. The streets we walked on were solid gold. I never got the name of this robed man. He led me to a huge house. It looked like a mansion, but bigger. Inside, it was even bigger than I thought was even possible. It went on for miles and miles. Soon after I was taken into this huge house, I woke up. I am thinking I am to keep living: to keep going on for miles and miles.

My Father's house has many rooms; if that
were not so, would I have told you that I am
going there to prepare a place for you?

And if I go and prepare a place for you, I
will come back and take you to be with me
that you also may be where I am.
John 14:2-3

I miss my brother every day. I also see it in my mom's face and eyes: she misses him as well. I worry about her being depressed. I do my best to get her out of her funk. Together we will get through this and carry on. Du would want us to. Life may not be fair, but God is fair. He knows what we have been through and I know He is going to make it up to us. We have faith in Him.

Duey Jordan and Colten Skinner sitting
in the lobby of the cancer center

LIFE'S A JOURNEY

Chapter 11

FRIENDS AND FUN

Blessings brighten when you count them.
Maltbie Davenport Babcock

I'VE BEEN BLESSED with a lot of good friends in my life. I have had a lot of fun along the way. One time I met a guy on our plane ride to Boston/Logan Airport. This guy was originally from the Boston area, but now lives in Kansas City, Missouri. He goes by the name of Boston Rob. Since he was from Boston, we got along well. We talked during the whole flight! It made the plane ride go by faster. I found out he had cancer. I told him that I had cancer, as well. We were flying in to Boston and staying in Foxboro to go to a Patriots game. He told my mom and I that he and a couple of his friends from Boston were going to have a Boston sports weekend. They were going to see hockey, basketball, baseball, and football games. I've been to one of these sporting events: baseball at Fenway Park. I was going to my first Patriots football game at Gillette Stadium. I would love to go to a Boston Bruins hockey and a Boston Celtics basketball game someday. When the plane landed we exchanged email addresses and he gave me his business card. Friends and new experiences are around every corner. All I have to do is open my eyes, be friendly, and say, "Hi."

I would challenge you to start up a conversation with the next person you meet. You never know what might happen. That next person you meet could be a blessing or you could be a blessing for them.

When we got off the plane we took a cab ride to our hotel at Patriot Place at Gillette Stadium in Foxboro, Massachusetts. Upon arrival at our hotel, I had a few surprises waiting for me from my good friend, Donna Spigarolo, and the New England Patriots. We had Patriots game tickets, my mom was given a Patriots bag, I had a Patriots hoodie, Patriots stocking cap, Patriots baseball cap, a Patriots football, and some Patriots collectibles. We had a perfect view of Gillette Stadium from our room. It was awesome!

My mom and I both were hungry. We found a restaurant nearby called, "Toby Keith's Bar and Grill." We decided we would try this place. The waitresses were all pretty and really nice. I did not know what to order so I asked our waitress what she liked. She said the boneless hot wings, so that's what I ordered. She was right! They were really good. When we were finished eating, my outgoing personality took over and before we left I asked our waitress if she would like to have her picture taken with me. I probably embarrassed my mom, but she *is* used to me interacting with strangers. After leaving the restaurant we literally went everywhere in Patriot Place. We walked from shop to shop, to the movie theaters, to the Hall at Patriot Place. If you remember earlier in this book, I told you that the Hall at Patriot Place was a big museum of Patriots collectables, Patriot Hall-of-Famers, interactives, and the Patriots Pro Shop for fans to get all the Patriots gear they need for the game, and then so much more! Everywhere I went I was talking to someone about either the Red Sox or the Patriots. I felt like I had been living in this area my whole life. It was my home away from home! At least for this weekend.

I got to meet in person another friend that I had previously friended online, Tommy Barnard Jr. He is a Boston sports fan like myself. He just has an advantage; he lives out there.

Tommy Barnard, Jr. and Colten Skinner in Boston, Massachusetts

The next day was game day, but this was not a normal game. It was the Crucial Catch game. My mom and I both got to go to a tailgate party, but this was not a normal tailgate party. The tailgate party you would think of has grilling going on and football fans of both teams. The tailgate party my mom and I got to go to had a lot of fans too, but was exclusively for cancer patients/survivors and their caregivers. We were all in a big room together and served an array of food and drinks. The food ranged from hot dogs to steak and everything in between. It was a great time talking with other cancer survivors. We met and hung out with two ladies that were really nice and fun. I wish I had gotten their emails. When everyone was finished eating and visiting it was time to head back to Gillette Stadium. We were taken into the tunnel to go on the field. While we were waiting I got pictures with some of the Patriots cheerleaders. Somebody had to do it, so why not me! When it was time to go on the field I was so excited and pumped I started waving to the crowd. Some were paying attention and waved back. We were taken to the Patriots sideline until after the National Anthem. At the end of the National Anthem we were escorted to the center of the field in a line by rows to form a heart, three rows deep. We were all color coordinated with our shirts being the colors of the different cancers. My shirt was purple for cancer in general and for my brother's pancreatic cancer.

While we were all making the shape of a heart on the field, one of the Patriots cheerleaders, Morgan Dzicek, was singing a beautiful and emotional song. She had a great voice and it was the perfect song for that night since it was celebrating all

Kim and Colten Skinner on the Patriot logo at
Gillette Stadium in Foxboro, Massachusetts

the cancer survivors. Even though I did not get to meet her (I would have liked to though) I had a connection with her. We were both strong cancer survivors. Morgan Dzicek was diagnosed with cancer when she was 13-years-old. Over the course of four years, she battled the effects of a tumor behind her left eye as she worked her way through high school, all the while staying focused on her love of music. Morgan wrote the song, "Every Step of the Way." I encourage you to go listen to this song. Maybe it will speak to you like it does me. Our seats at the Patriots game that night were awesome! They were in between the field goal posts. I was so excited after every Patriots touchdown I would high-five everyone around me. There was lots of screaming and hollering! When my favorite player, quarterback Tom Brady, ran it in for a touchdown, I really got loud! I mean really loud! The end zone was right below us.

Chapter 12

TB12, The G.O.A.T.

I HAVE BEEN blessed with another one of my dreams that I had growing up come true. In this chapter you will see why you should never give up on your dreams; they can come true! The second time that I was out in Boston for Red Sox games, I went with Kim Marshall, Stan Hudson, and my mom. This time was much like my first trip to the Boston/Foxboro area meeting the players. However, this time instead of Red Sox players, I got to meet Patriots players. A huge surprise awaited me at the end of my meeting with all the Patriots players that I would have never imagined and I never will forget. When we got to Gillette Stadium, we were taken on the field, in the press box, locker rooms (home and visitors), team kitchen, just about everywhere. I did not know there was a camera crew following us until we got in the Patriots locker room. Who knows how long they had been following us. I had no clue as to why these cameras were following us, but I soon found out. When we were finished touring the entire stadium we stopped in the tunnel. Everyone stepped away from me. I did not know what was going to happen next. I sat there for a few minutes then I saw number "87", Rob Gronkowski (Gronk) coming towards me. I yelled, "Gronk." He came over and we talked for a bit. Then, all the other players came to talk to me. I got to shake their hands and they all introduced themselves. I got all their autographs on a football given to me by Donna. However, I did not get to meet the one player that I had dreamed of meeting since I was a kid, Tom Brady. That was okay though, this day could not get any better, or could it? Then, all of a sudden, I saw him walking down the tunnel. There he was! The one and only, Tom Brady! I was so excited I felt like a little kid on Christmas morning. My mom says I said "Tom" about five times before he got to me. I probably did, but I sure do not remember saying that. I was in shock. Tom Brady was right next to me. We got to talk for quite a while before sadly it was time for us to go to the airport to come home. I still talk about the day that I, Colten Skinner, got to meet the New England Patriots, starting quarterback, #12 Tom Brady at Gillette Stadium in Foxboro, Massachusetts!

For those of you who do not know, I am a huge Tom Brady fan. Some information and history on Tom Brady. Thomas Edward Patrick Brady Jr. (born August 3, 1977) is now a quarterback for the Tampa Bay Buccaneers in the National Football League (NFL). He spent the first 20 seasons of his career with the New England Patriots, playing in nine Super Bowls and winning six of them (XXXVI, XXXVIII, XXXIX, XLIX, LI, and LIII), both of which are the most of any player in NFL history. He has won a record four Super Bowl MVP awards (XXXVI, XXXVIII, XLIX, and LI) as well as three NFL MVP awards (2007, 2010, 2017). Because of his numerous records and accolades, many sports writers, commentators, and players consider Brady to be the greatest quarterback of all time. He is the G.O.A.T. (Greatest of All Time). He played college football for the Wolverines at the University of Michigan. Brady was drafted 199th overall by the New England Patriots in the sixth round of the 2000 NFL Draft. Due to his late selection, Brady is considered by some to be the biggest "steal" in the history of the NFL Draft. He went on to become the team's starting quarterback in his second season (2002) after an injury to Drew Bledsoe. Brady played for the Patriots for 20 seasons, which is the NFL record for seasons as quarterback with one team. Now he is a member of the Tampa Bay Buccaneers or "Tompa Bay" in Tampa Bay, Florida. He plans to retire after his age 45 season. Tom Brady has two quotes that I really like. The first one is, "If you don't believe in yourself why is anyone else going to believe in you?" I love this quote because it tells me never to be afraid to try. If I do not believe I can, then I can't. It also reminds me that I can do anything if I just put my mind to it. Henry Ford once said; "Whether you think you can or think you can't, you're right." The second quote from Tom Brady is, "Sometimes some of the toughest things you deal with end up being the best things because you realize the people that you can rely on, love you and support you through it." I like this quote because even in your darkest times, you can always rely on family and friends to lift you up.

Chapter 13

AMERICAN CANCER SOCIETY

I'M VERY ACTIVE in cancer research funding organizations and the fight against cancer. For those who have not heard of American Cancer Society (ACS), it is a great organization. Whether you've recently been diagnosed, are currently going through treatment, or are caring for a loved one with cancer, ACS can provide you with information, day-to-day help, and emotional support. From free lodging and transportation to help making decisions about your care, they offer programs, services, and resources. They are there 24 hours a day, 7 days a week, to help guide you through your cancer journey. American Cancer Society is able to provide these services because of their numerous fund-raising events throughout the year. Their main fundraising event is Relay for Life. The Relay for Life event has several different teams that participate in this night of inspiration and fun. I've been relaying since I was diagnosed with my cancer. I started my own team, Colten's Crusaders Against Cancer, in memory and honor of my brother, Duey Jordan Skinner, who passed away March 26, 2018, just 14 days after my birthday. This was hard because it was supposed to be a happy time... Spring. A season of rebirth new life. Not the death of my brother. So a few days later, I decided to do something new: I started up my own Relay for Life team - Colten's Crusaders Against Cancer. I am so excited and blessed by my team members and all the support we have been given. I received honors for raising the most money during this Relay for Life event and earned Gold Team status in my first year of organizing my team in 2018. In the second year of having my team, my mom and I were asked to speak and tell my cancer story at the Jersey/Greene County Relay for Life.

In early spring of 2019, I entered a contest that ACS and the St. Louis Cardinals were hosting at Busch Stadium in St. Louis Missouri called "Survivor Starting Line-up." It was just like a baseball team's Line-up Card. The "Survivor Starting Line-up" consisted of nine positions: pitcher, catcher, first baseman, second baseman, third baseman, shortstop, left fielder, center fielder, and a right fielder. I was named to be shortstop and Ambassador for the Day at the ballpark. There were nine of us picked for this amazing honor; five cancer survivors/patients from Missouri and four cancer survivors/patients from Illinois. A couple of weeks before the "Survivor Starting Line-up" game, all nine of us got an exclusive VIP trip to Busch Stadium and gifts along the way. On the field at Busch Stadium, we got to meet one of the Cardinals players, second baseman, Kolten Wong. He spoke to us about the journey with his mom having breast cancer in 2013. It was a great day from start to finish.

Kim Marshall, Glenda Gray, Brenda Skinner, Eric Decker, Kelley Ingram, Dawn Dunham, Kevin Schroeder, Carla Brady, Jerry Dolan, Brad Hagen, Buford Conrad, Duey L. Skinner, Duey D. Skinner (dad), Colten Skinner, and Kim Skinner (mom) at the fish fry fundraiser for Colten's Crusaders Against Cancer

Kim Marshall, Kim Skinner, Alanna Buis, Josh Buis, Dawn Dunham, Carla Brady, Kaye Buis, Stan Hudson, Colten Skinner, and Tim Buis at Relay for Life in Jerseyville, Illinois

Colten Skinner with Kolten Wong and the
"Survivor Starting Line-up" members

There were two separate survivor games. The Illinois game
was first then the Missouri game followed at a later date. I'm
only going to elaborate on the Illinois game. The four cancer
survivors/patients from Illinois had to arrive at Busch Stadium
early to go over our duties/responsibilities. We each got to escort two current and\or former Cardinals players to their autograph booths. The four cancer survivors/patients from Illinois
"Survivor Starting Line-up" had one more special incentive.

I had to sell a certain number of tickets to get the amazing opportunity to deliver the game ball. Guess what! I did it! I sold the tickets and I got to deliver the game ball! I was nervous leading up to this. There was a lot of pressure on me not to drop the ball until I got to the pitcher's mound. Not to mention, I would be the very first person to deliver the game ball. You may or may not know this, but I like the flare for the dramatic. On the way back from taking the baseball to the pitcher's mound I raised my arms in the air. The crowd yelled and cheered for me. I think the crowd fueled me because when I stopped I could tell they wanted more. This time when I raised my arms up the Cardinals mascot, "Fredbird," grabbed my right arm and we held our arms up in the air for several seconds. The cameraman videoed us and had me up on the big screen. After my ten seconds of fame were over, it was time to head back to my seat for the game. I guess I had a pretty good day. Who am I kidding? I had a GREAT DAY! I met a lot of new friends, got to escort and talk with Cardinals' players, and oh yeah, I just made HISTORY!

If you look at what you have in life, you'll always have more. If you look at what you don't have in life, you'll never have enough.
Oprah Winfrey

Kim and Colten Skinner with St. Louis Cardinals' mascot,
Fredbird, after delivering the game ball – making history

Chapter 14

A Super Experience

MY FRIENDS FROM Baltimore, Maryland, Mike and Tammi Miller, get to go to the Super Bowl each year. Mike works for the National Football League (NFL). The 2019 was different for us all and I will never forget it.

Super Bowl 53, also known as Super Bowl LIII, was scheduled for Sunday, February 3, 2019, in Atlanta's Mercedes-Benz Stadium, home to the NFL's Atlanta Falcons. My favorite football team the New England Patriots were playing in there 11th Super Bowl and 9th under quarterback Tom Brady's leadership. I wanted to go to Atlanta for Super Bowl LIII so bad that I would enter a lot of contests trying to win tickets. The keyword being *trying*. I would try seven different contests, but sadly, no luck. I was planning on watching and cheering on my Patriots from home, on the couch, like always.

Lindsay, Mike, and Katie Miller and Colten
Skinner getting ready for the Super Bowl

Little did I know, that all would change. A couple of weeks before the big game, my mom got a call at work from our friend, Tammi Miller. She said, "Mike and I would like to give Colten my ticket to the Super Bowl in Atlanta, just don't tell him." My mom was totally caught off guard. She never expected this. Tammi told her to hold off on booking airfare until she was able to secure my mom and I a hotel room. Tammi called my mom at work the following Monday afternoon, six days before the Big Game to let her know that Mike was able to get through to the NFL Fan Experiences for Super Bowl LIII - Management Council and get us a room at the hotel where they were staying. This was awesome! There were Hall of Famers staying there, as well. My mom immediately reserved our flights to Atlanta for Super Bowl LIII. We were all set. The thing was, I still had no clue another one of my dreams was about to come true. My mom kept it a secret. I would call the Millers on Tuesday evening (as I did every year) since they were leaving Wednesday for Atlanta. We talked about the game and I told them to be sure to cheer on my PATRIOTS! Mike said, "You can cheer them on." I told him I would be, but I want you guys to because you will be at the game. He then said, "You will, too." There was a silence. I was at a loss for words. If you know me, you know this is unusual. Mike broke the silence, "Colten, you will be cheering on Tom Brady and your Patriots next to me at the game." Silence again. This was out of the ordinary as I never have a loss for words. I was speechless. I was in shock! Was I being punk'd? No! It was for real. I would be going to the Super Bowl! Yes! Me, Colten Skinner, was going to the Super Bowl! Our conversation soon started back up again. I was so very excited! I could not believe I was actually going to the Super Bowl. I counted down the days/hours until my mom and I would finally leave for Atlanta, the site of Super Bowl LIII. Upon arrival at the hotel, the Miller family were waiting for us. We talked and caught up some. Then we went out to eat dinner. When we got back to our hotel we saw a few Hall of Famers and I got some pictures with them. The next day, one day before the big game, we went to the Super Bowl Experience. The Super Bowl Experience is a great time! It has everything for every NFL fan from player sightings to fun interactives. I decided that I would try one of the interactives. This one was based on the NFL Draft. It was cool because it was like you were getting drafted. When it came time for my pick, the announcer said, "The New England Patriots select cornerback/free safety, Colten, don't call me Leonard, Skinner." This was so much fun. The next day was the main event: The Super Bowl. The morning of the game, all six of us, the Millers, my mom and I, got to have brunch with some retired players and people Mike knew from attending previous games. When we finished eating, Mike, Lindsay, Katie, and I headed to a tailgate party while my mom and Tammi stayed behind and had a girl's day. The tailgate party was a fun time! There were concerts, pictures with cheerleaders, food/drinks overall a great time. I knew an even better time was right around the corner though. We left the tailgate party a little early to head to the stadium to find our seats. We had awesome seats to cheer on the Pats. And cheer I did! Mike went to get some food while I stayed put and just took it all in. I could not believe I was at the Super Bowl. It was a once in a lifetime kind of thing. This would probably never happen again, I told myself. When the game started I was very loud. On every first down the Patriots made I got louder. It was a very tight game. The final score ended up 13-3 in favor of the Patriots. When Tom Brady threw the football deep to Gronk and he caught it on the four-yard line, I lost my mind. I went absolutely insane! After the game, the elevator was out of order. Oh no! Well, it wasn't so bad. An usher escorted us out, so Mike, Katie, Lindsay, and I got to see other parts of the stadium that we wouldn't have otherwise. I guess you could say we went behind the scenes. On the way out I saw Dont'a Hightower, a linebacker (LB) for the Patriots, and said, "Champions baby!" to him and he replied, "Yes, ain't it sweet!" Out in the parking lot on the way to the bus, Mike and I were singing and being loud. We were just being crazy. I know we had to embarrass Katie and Lindsay because they were walking several feet behind us. What can I say? I was excited! Oh yeah, was I ever! When we got back to the hotel I was still pumped and loud. I met tons of new friends while I was in Atlanta. I got the new name of "Big Deal." I would say I had a pretty awesome three days in Atlanta for the Super Bowl. I mean just going to the Super Bowl in its self is unbelievable. Seeing your favorite team play and win is a dream come true!

Colten Skinner finally makes it to the Super Bowl

Chapter 15

FRIENDS AND FAMILY ARE EVERYTHING

Life is short, don't waste time worrying about what people think of you. Hold on to the ones that care, because in the end, they will be the only ones there.
Unknown

I HAVE MADE a lot of friends that have been blessings in my life. Real blessings begin with family. What is a family? A family can be different for every one of us. Family can consist of one or two parents, grandparents, siblings, aunts, uncles, cousins, and even friends. I have the family that I live with, my mom and granny. My mom is my rock. She is always there when I need her to be. I love her!

Kim (mom) and Colten Skinner

I love both my parents, but in different ways. My dad was and still is on the road working a lot. We make the most out of what time we have together. Whether it's going out to my grandparents' house or just going for a ride, we always have a good time. Unlike my mom, I do not get to see him every day. We talk as often as we can. When I was a kid, I remember going to Texas with him in his tractor trailer truck. We would run over really big spiders in the road. This was really fun and exciting for me. On our way home there was a museum of amazing and frightening animals. We got to stop and go in. I got to see the world's largest snake. I also saw a three-legged goat. This place was pretty awesome!

When Du and I were young, all four of us went in dad's tractor trailer truck to visit my Aunt Kim and my Uncle Jeff at their condo in Daytona, Florida. I went for trips as often as I could.

Duey D.(dad) and Colten Skinner

Family means a group of people who genuinely love, trust, care about, and look out for each other. A real family bond cannot be broken by any means.

On my mom's side of my family I have Granny; Aunt Dawn; Uncle Jimmy and Aunt Michelle, my two cousins, Owen and Eli.

Granny, Colten, Aunt Michelle, Kim (mom),
Uncle Jimmy, Aunt Dawn, Eli and Owen

On my dad's side of the family I have Grandma and
Grandpa; Aunt Kim and Uncle Jeff; Aunt Brenda. I also have
my cousins Brad and Nicole and their daughters: Maddie,
Nora, and Charlotte; Tara and Steve and their children: Coby,
Dylan and Keely; Katelyn and Tom; Meghan and Rob; and
Danah.

Coby, Aunt Kim, Maddie, Uncle Jeff, Nicole, Brad, Nora, Grandma, Steve, Tara, Colten, Danah, Tom, Katelyn, Rob, Meghan, Grandpa, Charlotte, Dylan, Aunt Brenda, Keely, and Duey D. (dad)

<u>Family</u>

A little bit of crazy

A little bit of loud

A whole lot of love

Also, I have my church family at First Baptist Church. I have been going to First Baptist Church since I was a little kid. You would say I have grown spiritually there. I had Christian leaders at church who taught me how to be strong in my faith and to turn my worries over to my Lord and Savior Jesus Christ. I know to pray more and worry less. If you do not have family and friends, you have nothing. Through the hard times you can always count on family and friends to be right there to comfort you and you are there for them, as well.

The church is not a select circle of the immaculate, but a home where the outcast may come in. It is not a palace with gate attendants and challenging sentinels along the entrance-ways holding off at arm's-length the stranger, but rather a hospital where the broken-hearted may be healed, and where all the weary and troubled may find rest and take counsel together.
James H. Aughey

Brayden Morris and I have been best friends since the 3rd grade when he moved to Jerseyville, Illinois from Texas. We have been through a lot together - from the bad times to the good times. We have always been there for each other. I cannot drive so he would take me anywhere I wanted to go, well, most of the time he would take me. When we were younger Brayden and I used to go out to my grandma and grandpa's house. They live out in the country. We would ride around in our go-carts for hours. We got to spend the night out there, too. My grandparents have a finished basement, so when Brayden and I stayed, this is where we got to sleep. Sleep? Yes, we did get some sleep, but most of the night was spent eating pizza, drinking soda, and playing video games. What a great friend I have! I guess you could say he is part of my family.

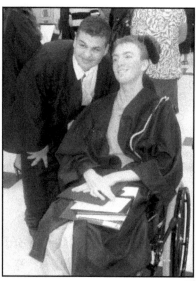

Brayden Morris and
Colten Skinner at high
school graduation

Brayden Morris and
Colten Skinner

*A friend is someone who knows all
about you and still loves you.*
Elbert Hubbard.

Chapter 16

ACCOMPLISHMENTS

I MISSED QUITE a bit of my senior year in high school because of being in the hospital. I still did win Homecoming King and I graduated! At my high school graduation, when my name was called, I got a standing ovation. This brought a tear to my eye and gave me chills. The good kind of tears and chills. This was because graduating was a huge accomplishment in itself, but everyone knew that beating cancer was bigger. Upon graduation from Jersey Community High School, I started college at Lewis and Clark Community College and then Missouri Baptist University. My schooling had taken me longer than the usual four years. I had a big bump in the road, cancer. My cancer treatments derailed me from finishing on schedule. Being blessed by the understanding of my teachers/instructors, my hard work and determination, I received a Bachelor of Science Degree with a Major in Management and a Minor in Business Administration.

Colten Skinner with his Bachelor of Science Degree

I was also chosen as one of two Business Students of the Year. I am still looking for that perfect job. My ideal job would be something in a hospital with cancer patients. Since I had cancer I think I would have some good insight and would be able to relate with the patients. My dream job would be something in the NFL with the Kraft Group for the New England Patriots. I have applied a couple times with no luck. I am not going to give up. When God shuts one door it does not mean you are done. It just means He has something bigger and better for you behind another door that He will open.

When something bad happens you have three choices:
You can let it define you, let it destroy
you, or let it strengthen you.
Theodor Seuss Geisel

Epilogue...

IN THIS BOOK you have seen how God has taken some of my hardships and turned them into countless blessings. This was possible through people I have met. Like in the movie, *Forest Gump*, Tom Hanks character says, "Life is like a box of chocolates. You don't know what you're going to get." This quote is exactly right. You don't know what you will get next. There is no way to know what life has in store for you. You may think these people just came into my life by chance, a coincidence per se, but I *know* it was the works of God. God works in mysterious ways! Life is a mystery. We should be thankful for each and every day we have. Praise God through whom all blessings flow! I feel as if the hardships that we are going through are to strengthen our faith and to make us more like Christ. With that being said I ask you what does the word *life* mean to you? Stop for a moment and look around. Maybe it is time you look at your life.

A line from the song, "Keep Me in the Moment" by Jeremy Camp, sums up how we should live each moment of our life:

Oh Lord
Keep me in the moment
Help me live
With my eyes wide open
'Cause I don't wanna miss
What You have for me

Colten Skinner in the garden at St. Louis Children's Hospital

About the Author...

Colten J. Skinner lives in Jerseyville, Illinois. He is a member of First Baptist Church in Jerseyville where he serves as a Deacon. He is an assistant to the youth director at his church. He is a committee member of Kids Shouldn't Have Cancer Foundation where he is a sales and marketing volunteer. He is also a team captain (Colten's Crusaders Against Cancer) for Relay for Life of Jersey & Greene Counties in memory\ honor of his brother, Duey Jordan who died from pancreatic cancer. Colten has a Bachelor of Science Degree with a Major in Management, Minor in Business Administration, and Certificates of Proficiency.

"Stronger" by Mandisa
From *What if we were Real* (2011) on Sparrow Records

Hey, heard you were up all night
Thinking about how your world ain't right
And you wonder if things will ever get better
And you're asking, why is it always raining on you
When all you want is just a little good news
Instead of standing there stuck out in the weather
Oh, don't hang your head
It's gonna end
God's right there
Even if it's hard to see Him
I promise you that He still cares
When the waves are taking you under
Hold on just a little bit longer
He knows that this is gonna make you stronger, stronger
The pain ain't gonna last forever
And things can only get better
Believe me
This is gonna make you stronger
Gonna make you stronger, stronger, stronger
Believe me, this is gonna make you
Try and do the best you can
Hold on and let Him hold your hand
Go on and fall into the arms of Jesus
Oh, lift your head it's gonna end
God's right there
Even when you just can't feel Him

I promise you that He still cares
When the waves are taking you under
Hold on just a little bit longer
He knows that this is gonna make you stronger, stronger
The pain ain't gonna last forever
Things can only get better
Believe me
This is gonna make you stronger
'Cause if He started this work in your life
He will be faithful to complete it
If only you believe it
He knows how much it hurts
And I'm sure that He's gonna help you get through this
When the waves are taking you under
Hold on just a little bit longer
He knows that this is gonna make you stronger, stronger
The pain ain't gonna last forever
Things can only get better
Believe me
This is gonna make you stronger
gonna make you stronger, stronger, stronger
This is gonna make you stronger
Gonna make you stronger, stronger, stronger
Believe me
Only gonna make you stronger

Don't look at how big your problems are.
Look at how big your God is.
Joel Osteen

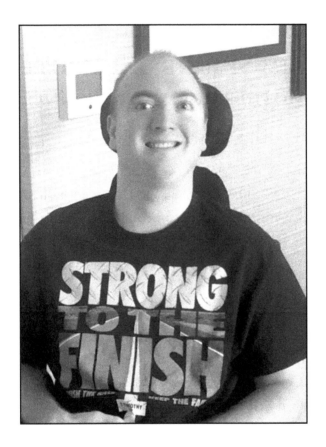

I have been blessed with so much love and support from all my family and friends. I do not know where I would be today without them. You truly don't know what you have until you take a break and look at your life.

Kim Skinner's Tribute
(Mother of Colten Skinner)

Being the mother of Colten and Duey Jordan, in one hand is a challenge at times, in the other it is the **Greatest Blessing** of my life. This book, written by my youngest son, Colten, is all about hardships he has faced and how he has been blessed in return.

At a young age, Colten accepted his physical challenge and never looked at himself as disabled, but rather as abled. He has always been determined to be like everyone else. Well, not exactly! Colten isn't satisfied with being like everyone else and just fitting in. He strives to, and takes pride in, standing out in the crowd.

Colten's outgoing personality and sense of humor are traits that make him stand out. They are also the very traits that make him so likeable. He considers everyone he meets a friend. These friends have been blessings and have blessed Colten, as well as, myself over the years. Colten has never met a stranger. He looks at them as friends he has yet to meet. If you ever meet Colten, he is someone that you will not soon forget.

Caring, grateful, kind, funny, compassionate, ambitious, thoughtful, and nonjudgmental are just a few words that come to mind when I think of my son. I am so extremely proud of him. He has grown to be a wonderful young man, a faithful servant of the Lord, and my rock.

Over the years I have been commended on how well I take care of my two sons. Contrary, they take care of me. They inspire me each and every day to be the best version of myself.

Congratulations on your first book! May God Bless You Today and Always!

With All My Love,

Mom

Testimonials

There will never be another person quite like Colten Skinner. Things aren't always easy but you can't tell this guy, "No!" I have known Colten since he was very young. We met at church. Even at a young age it was apparent there was not anything Colten wasn't going to accomplish. We have been involved in many church and community fundraising events. He always wants to help everyone else. When the odds are against him, he really digs in and makes it happen. Colten is such a blessing and always makes me smile. May God bless him for writing this book.

Kim Marshall, Friend

When it comes to Colten Skinner there are plenty of things that come to mind but two words stand out more than most. I have been best friends with Colten since the 3rd grade and when I think of Colten I think of the words gifted and strong-willed. Colten started life with a disadvantage and it has not slowed him down one bit. Colten has had many challenges in his life and every single one he's come out on top just like any strong-willed person would. Colten has always used his life challenges to inspire other people along the way and no challenge you put in front of him is big enough. Colten has kept his faith in God since day one and at times, even though he has been discouraged, he has never been defeated and that is where gifted comes into play. Colten has always been gifted with the ability to make everyone and everything around him better. Colten has a gift to encourage those who surround him to be better people and has always encouraged people to do more for those who may not have as much. Colten has never let his disability stop his gift to give back to people, whether it be through donations or speaking to raise money through charities. If you are lucky enough to know Colten, then you know that the moment Colten came into your life, you were gifted with a strong-willed, caring human being. Colten will always be my best friend and someone that I look up to and inspires me to be the best version of myself every day.

Brayden Morris, Best Friend

Colten Skinner has touched the hearts and souls of all who know him. His compassion, determination, and faith have inspired him to excel in spite of his physical limitations. Colten is a devoted son and brother and has a "heart of gold." I admire his quick wit and sense of humor. His accomplishments have been amazing. Colten has persevered against all odds and has been both a blessing and an inspiration to both young and old alike. It has been a joy and a privilege to acknowledge him as one of the most outstanding young men I have ever known and I congratulate him on his book.

Linda J. Crotchett
Jersey County Clerk, Retired